Jesus Loves the Little Children

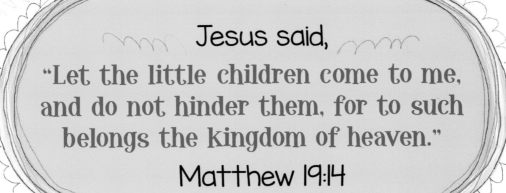

Jesus said,

"Let the little children come to me, and do not hinder them, for to such belongs the kingdom of heaven."

Matthew 19:14

By Dallas and Amanda Jenkins

Illustrated by Kristen Hendricks

BEAVER'S POND PRESS
SAINT PAUL

Written by Dallas and Amanda Jenkins
Illustration and design by Kristen Hendricks
Edited by Lily Coyle
File production by Dan Pitts

ISBN 13: 978-1-64343-838-2
Library of Congress Catalog Number: 2020919113
Printed in India
Fourth Printing: 2022
25 24 23 22   7 6 5 4

Beaver's Pond Press
939 Seventh Street West
Saint Paul, MN 55102
(952) 829-8818
www.BeaversPondPress.com

To order more of this book, visit: thechosen.tv/store

JOSHUA AND ABIGAIL WERE FRIENDS.

Joshua was shy, which meant he didn't talk much.
Especially to new people.

ABIGAIL TALKED A LOT.

A LOT.

One day, while Abigail was playing in the fields outside her village, she came across a campsite.

There was a tent and a fire, a little bit of food, and some tools.

AND TOYS.

There were long smooth spoons,
a top for spinning, a rowboat,
and a miniature horse. They were all
carved out of wood and just the
right size for Abigail's doll.

But playtime was interrupted by
the sound of footsteps, so Abi ran
home before being discovered.

Or so she thought.

The next day,

Abigail wanted to return to the campsite.

Only this time she brought Joshua.

"And there was one tool I've never seen before.
I don't know what it's for—I think he's building stuff.
There were toys and food too—
but I didn't take any, because that would be wrong.
If he comes again this time, should we say something?
I think if you are with me, it's okay.
I didn't see a sword or anything.

DO YOU HAVE A SWORD?

Oh—we're almost there. Walk faster, Joshua!"

When the children arrived, there was a man sitting in front of his lunch. He was praying.

"Blessed are you, Lord our God, King of the Universe, who gives us bread from heaven."

"And I pray that if there are ever two children who visit my home here, you will give them the courage to say shalom so that they know they don't have to be afraid. Amen."

Abigail and Joshua didn't know whether to say hello or run away.

Suddenly, the man made a

REALLY SILLY SOUND.

And then another.

And another.

Abigail and Joshua
couldn't help
but laugh.

"Greetings, children. You were wise
to bring your friend this time, and he was brave to come."

"SO WHAT ARE YOU DOING HERE?"

"WHERE ARE YOU FROM?"

"WHAT'S THE WOOD FOR?"

"ARE YOU A CARPENTER?"

"WHAT DO YOU BUILD?"

"MY FAMILY ISN'T WEALTHY."

"I DON'T KNOW ABOUT THAT."

"OK—TIME TO GO!"

"I'm visiting for a time."

"Nazareth."

"I'm building something."

"I am. I build all kinds of things."

"Wealthy people love decorations and also toys for their children."

"Many times that's better."

Jesus laughed. "You will."

Jesus laughed again.

BECAUSE ABIGAIL TALKED A LOT.

The next morning, Abigail
returned to the campsite again,

ONLY

THIS

TIME

she brought a
whole group of
kids with her.

"You couldn't have waited half an hour, eh?"

Jesus asked before opening his eyes.

"Can we be around today?
These are my friends. And Joshua again."

"Shalom, Abigail's friends. And Joshua again."

"Yes, I suppose you can be around today,"
Jesus said. "But I have some work to do.
You might have to help."

The children were quick to agree.
Jesus was as kind and curious
as Abi had said.

So why are you living in a tent?
My home is many places.
Do you have friends?
A few, and more to come.
How much longer will you stay here?
Until it is time for me to go.
When's that?
I have some work to do here.
And some people to meet.

"I STILL DON'T UNDERSTAND,"
ABIGAIL SAID.
"WHY ARE YOU HERE?"

"Because I have a much larger job than being a carpenter. And you are more than just children who play and go to school. You are to show love to one another, to share God's Word, and most important . . . to love who?"

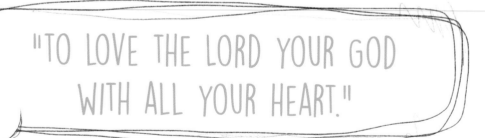

"TO LOVE THE LORD YOUR GOD WITH ALL YOUR HEART."

"Very good, Joshua the Brave."

"So I will be doing my work in MANY places . . .
the Spirit of the Lord is upon me.

He has anointed me to bring good news to the poor, to heal the brokenhearted, and to proclaim freedom to the captives."

The next day, the children came back to spend more time with Jesus.

And the next day. AND THE NEXT.

They loved walking with him.

They loved sitting with him. They loved talking to him—especially Abigail.

AND THEY LOVED LISTENING TO JESUS TALK.

"Children," Jesus said as he gathered his little friends close.

"Soon it will be time for me to go and to do the work God has prepared for me."

"But I have loved spending this time with you—

you are all so very special.

I hope that my next students ask the same questions that you do, and that they listen to my answers.

And I hope that when the time comes, they will tell others about me—like you have, Abigail."

When Abi returned to the campsite the following morning, the tent, food, tools, and toys were gone.

But Jesus had left something behind.

Dear Abigail,
I'm going now to do my work in other places, but I will miss hearing you talk. I made this for you.

You and your friends were the reason I came.